CAN'T NOT WON'T

Can't Not Won't

A Story About A Child Who
Couldn't Go To School

Written and illustrated by

Eliza Fricker

Guidance and Thoughts for Schools and Professionals by Sue Moon
Reflections for Schools and Professionals by Tom Vodden

Jessica Kingsley Publishers
London and Philadelphia

First published in Great Britain in 2023 by Jessica Kingsley Publishers
An imprint of Hodder & Stoughton Ltd
An Hachette Company

1

A CIP catalogue record for this title is available from the British Library
and the Library of Congress

ISBN 978 1 83997 520 2
eISBN 978 1 83997 521 9

Printed and bound in Great Britain by TJ Books Limited

Jessica Kingsley Publishers' policy is to use papers that are natural,
renewable and recyclable products and made from wood grown in
sustainable forests. The logging and manufacturing processes are expected
to conform to the environmental regulations of the country of origin.

Jessica Kingsley Publishers
Carmelite House
50 Victoria Embankment
London EC4Y 0DZ

www.jkp.com

To B, you make my heart swell with pride.

Acknowledgements

Thank you, Nonna, for your continually excellent and succinct summaries of often totally deranged scenarios and for listening when all I could do was cry.

To Dad for all those fun times we had mucking about at home growing up. These memories really helped me to keep pulling it out of the bag.

To my editor Lynda and everyone at JKP for your support.

To all my friends old and new who have been there.

I want to dedicate this book to all the families and children whom I have met, and will continue to meet, whose children try so very hard until they can't do it any more.

This is all our story.
This is for all of you.

Introduction

I started writing and drawing our experiences when my daughter was at home full time, unable to attend school. It began as a way for me to process our experiences of the previous eight years with the school system, something I couldn't have done at the time because most of those days were spent navigating and predicting hurdles and potential pitfalls; managing the distress and fallout of each school day would often take us beyond what would be deemed a respectable bedtime and that was before we started on meetings, emails, courses.

Drawing and writing while in slippers at home all day gave me more than just time to heal and process, it connected me with a whole community of families just like ours, whose children struggle with school every day. This was incredibly helpful because actually, when we were going through it all, we felt like we were the only people in the same boat. We were 'that family' with an enigma of a child, and I think I carried this with me for many years. 'Oh well, how can they help us? We are such an unusual case.'

In a way, this slightly fatalistic narrative was oddly comforting. When professionals were unable to help, I thought that they had never seen such a situation arise before because, after all, what child doesn't want to go to school? But now I know differently. There are so many of us who are still trying to get their children to attend every day, or who are quietly and shamefully dealing with the fallout from the impact of the school day at home. There are many more who (like us now) are finding that after years of our child struggling to attend school, and worrying we would be in trouble when they stopped, there were very few phone calls, emails or home visits when it actually happened. I learnt very quickly that when your child isn't in school it will go quiet on the communication front.

I also learnt, once we were home and without the daily pressures and distress, that I had been putting on a brave face at those school gates and that doing that for many years had taken its toll on my mental health.

I know now I was quite unwell, hiding this from most friends and other parents because, I mean, where do you start? And frankly, who wants to hear a story that rambles on across eight years, covering bureaucratic nightmares that even you can't keep track of?

Because these are systems that are not only utterly baffling and maddening, they are truly boring. I still can't read our Education, Health and Care Plan (EHCP) as it is written in language that is neither engaging nor reflective of my child.

I learnt that while most teachers and professionals we met were well-meaning, they were trapped by the same systems as we were. I wish they could have given us options, though. As well as more honesty, and more consistency of communication and relationships. That would have been better than departments and people you saw once and then never again.

And I really wish they hadn't given us so much positive spin, because this not only invalidated the reality of the misery we were in, it wasn't helpful when it came to preparing us for the future.

I wish I'd ducked out of the coffee mornings and parent class-es because I lost so much time and learnt nothing about the autistic experience, masking or monotropism. This would have been knowledge, this would have been empowering for my family, but instead the focus was always on managing behaviour. But I felt I couldn't skip these sessions or I'd be seen as a bad parent – and you do everything in your might not to be perceived as that when your child's attendance is below 90 per cent.

This is actually why I took up vacuuming during this time: because I didn't want people to think I was a failure (on a plus side, the house had never been tidier).

However, I did figure out that when I shouted, begged, cajoled and cried, I wasn't really listening to my daughter, I was listening to others instead – because I was worried and scared of what they might think of me, of all of us, because all children have to go school.

This is the hard bit. I learnt that when our children struggle, we risk breaking their trust. We watch their distress, listen to them late into the night and then the next day we make them go back to that place all over again. Back to school.

I know my story isn't the worst. I have heard what other families and children have gone through, experiences that are truly, truly dreadful, and no family should have to go through such upset.

It should be enough for any child to say or show that they are too unwell to go to school and then we should have options, choices, without needing to join waiting lists that stretch for years and years, or seek more appointments, more evidence.

I honestly think that if we had more flexibility, if we had safety, connections and strong relationships alongside learning, we would need fewer 'supports', EHCPs, expensive reports and court cases. We could have reduced wait times for appointments because we would have fewer children that needed to be 'fixed'. Right now, it is system of fitting in, with the onus all on the child, not the environment.

I think we as the adults still have a lot of learning to do.

We need to start with sorry: sorry this happened to you.

Sorry we didn't hear you.

I know you tried so hard, for so long.

Can't not won't.

Eighteen Months
We spent hours with friends and their babies in the park, eating sandwiches and playing on the swings

Thirteen Months
Your first proper walk in proper shoes

Fifteen Months
We didn't have much money but we did have nice days out

'Enjoy this time,
you'll never
get it back'

You struggled to settle at nursery

and apart from one intense friendship

you preferred to stay with your favourite nursery teacher

We only lived a few minutes' walk from the nursery but you would often cry all the way home...

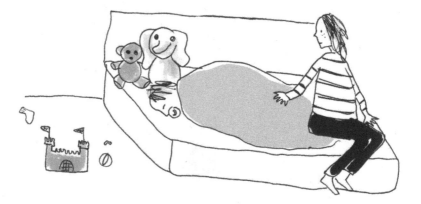

And then go straight to bed

'Maybe she's shy'

'That's what all children do, they play up to their parents and they are fine once you've gone'

When you started school this didn't get better, it got worse

You learnt ways to hold the handle of my bag so tight it was impossible to break away without hurting you...

You didn't want to do class assemblies and show what you'd done. You wanted to be with the teacher

'We are not sure
what else we
can do really'

Meanwhile, you went to the children's clinic for an assessment and two hours later you were diagnosed as autistic. They gave me some chewing gum grey sheets to take home

Two years, one month
You loved balloons, bubbles, soft toys, frogs and cats. We used to tip you upside down and tickle your chin and you would laugh hysterically

Second birthday
I made you a chocolate cake and we bought you an old Fisher Price till from Ebay

Two years and seven months.
You always loved dressing up, making dens and playing in cardboard boxes and still do

Ten months
Lazy weekends in pyjamas, eating pancakes and drinking cups of tea

'Is she high-functioning?'

'She doesn't
look autistic'

Now I got to go to other school buildings I'd never been to with other parents I'd never met.
I got instant coffee, biscuits and lanyards

Lots of the parents would be angry in those rooms and it made me feel awkward because I'd never met them before

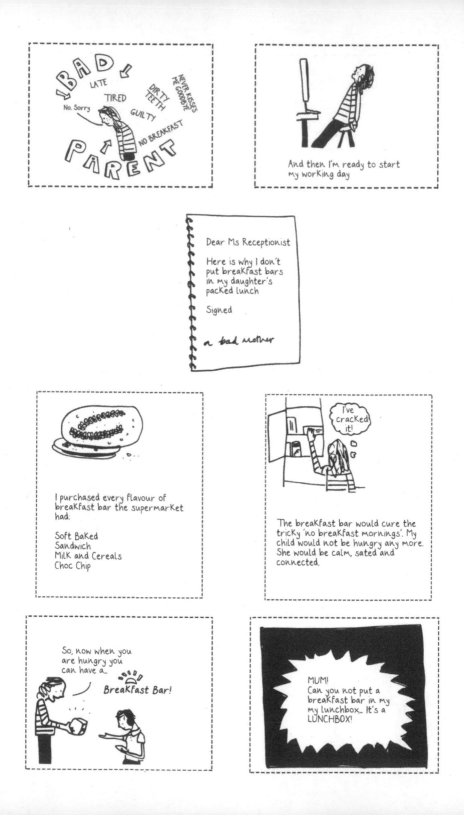

'No child "wants" to go to school'

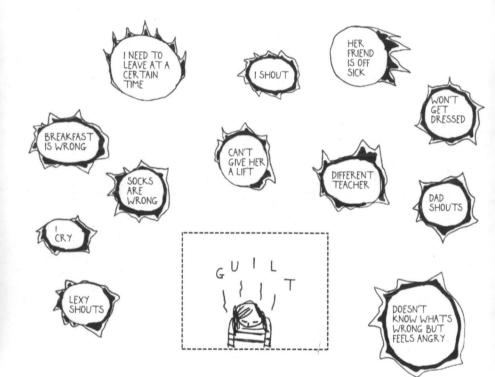

'She'll have to
learn to get
on with it'

A GOOD MORNING

'Have you tried lavender oil?'

Why we gave up homework fairly early on...

'Swimming is fun for the children, it's a break from the lessons'

Hours and hours later...

Back to the same shop (for the third time that week)

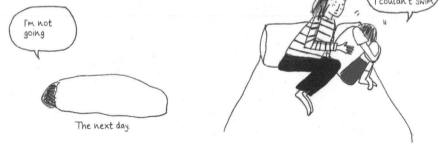

You only managed a few swimming lessons and then stopped being able to go. On the day of the last session after being distressed all morning you were finally able to tell me your class teacher had put you in with the younger children because you couldn't swim. You were the only child he did this to

'All children enjoy Sports Day, they get an ice pop'

'Have you tried
a whiteboard?'

You got the autism supports used for the autistic children in school

Including one called 'Just Right'

Our local authority used it with all ASC families

But you didn't need more laminated sheets of paper...

'In the blue'

You needed the right support for you

'She seems fine'

What did I do?

I went to meetings, I sat on small plastic chairs, I stuck visitor stickers on and signed in and out. I cried and got offered head tilts and non-absorbent tissues that didn't mop my snot or tears. I nodded along

How You Might React

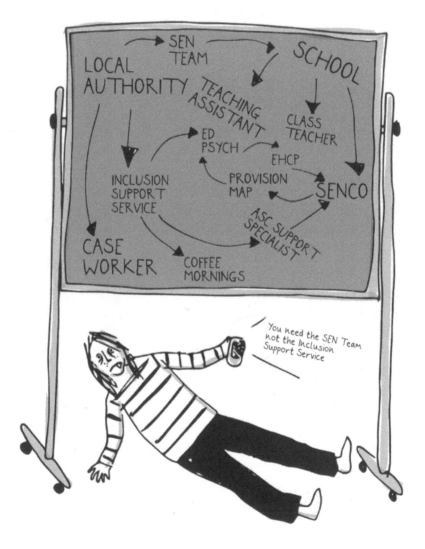

So many fragmented systems to navigate...

Sometimes I could deal with it all and other times it was just so tiring and overwhelming. I was trying to learn how this system worked as well as trying to help my child get through another day

Would I become the Stanley Green of our city?
I just wanted to watch telly and walk the dog

Sitting in sterile offices with tired, worn-out teachers who were sometimes kind and sometimes baffled.
They didn't know what to do and nor did we.
But I always thought, most have your best interest at heart.
I mean, they are teachers, right?

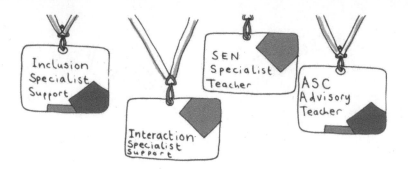

Not only was it complicated, the support felt so alien from real life...

I mean, who saw 'us'?

School

Home

'Do you think we need an EHCP?'

'No'

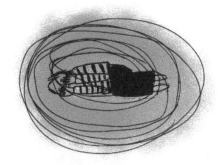

At home I sat with you for hours while you hid under the duvet.
I read and read to try and get you to sleep.
I lay in the dark biting the skin around my nails

The combination of guilt, frustration and anxiety led to increased vertigo attacks. Sometimes I would feel dizzy just thinking about all the worries and other times I had to lie in the dark for several hours waiting for it to subside

You can't
Keep making
allowances'

CLASS OF 2019

yearbook

Learn together~Achieve together

PERFECT MUM
75.2K followers on her lifestyle blog about her tidy home. Children always in matching outfits. Offers you her diet plan of nuts and steamed cabbage to help 'manage your child

BUSINESS MUM
Drops her children off at dawn to school for Breakfast Club. Picks them up at dusk from After School Club. Children are absolutely fine, well rounded individuals and do all their homework, attend all clubs. Wear full uniform

'Our Community'

ct Believe Excellence

HIPPY ART MUM
Looks after lots of children for everyone as well as her own. Ferries them all around, carries all their book bags and lunch boxes. After school snacks are all homemade. Goes away most weekends with lots of friends and kids. Never yawns

POSH MUM
Kids are always in creased uniforms, trousers that are too small and their hair is long and unkempt. Meets other mums every Friday for fizz

MISSING THE MARK
No one is sure what's going on with her and her child

You look at schools a year before they go to secondary school...

It seemed nice but I wasn't sure I had a lot to compare it to

I guess I did learn about different types of people...

And some life skills

We also had a tour for parents of Special Educational Needs Children...

It seemed nice...

But a lot can change in a year

And now our chosen school didn't seem so accommodating...

On the phone to our case worker

The transition plan with our school and secondary school didn't seem to be marrying up either...

So who was responsible for making a plan?

Other options...

I used to pass an old house on dog walks...

Sometimes I'd see some of the students and teachers in the park

But I never saw anyone outside the school

So when the local authority mentioned it I thought I should have a look...

On the day of the visit...

On the phone to my husband...

I'll skim over looking at Special Schools and even a trial session at one that ended after half an hour with an anxiety attack

Parents with autistic children were offered a six-week course on transitioning to secondary school

This was the Family Support Worker, who had visited us once...

She had talked a lot about girls' developing bodies during puberty and not looked me in the eyes

I managed one more week and then never went back

'They need to learn resilience'

Quality FIRST Teaching

Embed strategies into the classroom

ACCESS TO... A SENSORY DIET

DEVELOP AWARENESS ★OF★ Sensory Profile

TEACHER LED ACTIVITIES

March

Daily and embedded within the curriculum and the whole school day

ACCESS
WILL BENEFIT
REGULAR
APPROPRIATE
EMBED
STRATEGIES

Regular Access TO Appropriate SUPPORT

Meanwhile we finally got an Education, Health and Care Plan agreed. This was a legally binding document that oulined provision and a budget but I didn't understand most of what was written in it. It was full of phrases that I had never heard before

This is a
safeguarding
issue...

A member of
staff must be
with visitors
at all times

I'm sorry
you felt
upset, shall
we have a
chat, just
you and
me?

OKay

Meanwhile I got to meet the acclaimed Advisory Teacher for Inclusion.
(who came up with all these job titles??)

'Sometimes you've got to get tough or they just won't learn'

Falling apart but trying to keep it together

'Try not to be late
when you go to
secondary school'

Those last weeks of primary, we all scraped by.
That summer is still so hard to remember.
Yes, it was rough at primary, but the next place?
A school of thousands, with timetables, uniforms, rules?

The summer before secondary school my mum bought us
tickets to stay with friends in New York for my 40th birthday

Even though we were thousands of miles away in our favourite city I couldn't stop thinking about September

We did our favourite things but I felt tired and worried

How will she cope?

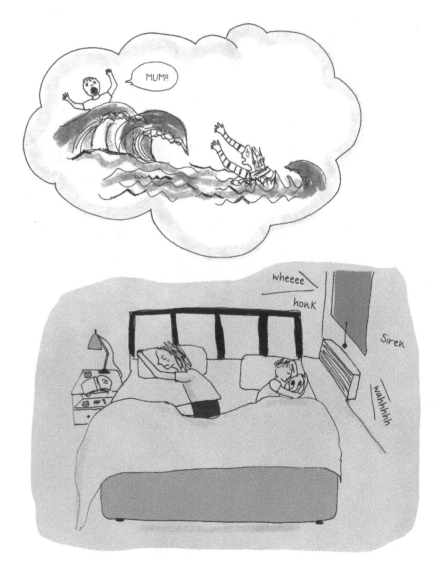

The nights were as noisy as the days and I slept fitfully, having horrible dreams

September 2019
First and only day of secondary school

'We are deeming
the day a success'

I would have thought it was a big deal
if a child was unable to go to school...

But it was weeks of a convoluted chain
of emails with no one making any decisions
or even checking in on us

Apart from one random phone call...

Who seemed to not know anything about our situation…

But as one of the few people to actually phone us
they got the full wrath of our misery and frustration

A few minutes later...

But I also worried if we didn't comply then we would get in trouble too...

The following week...

Twenty minutes later

She was right

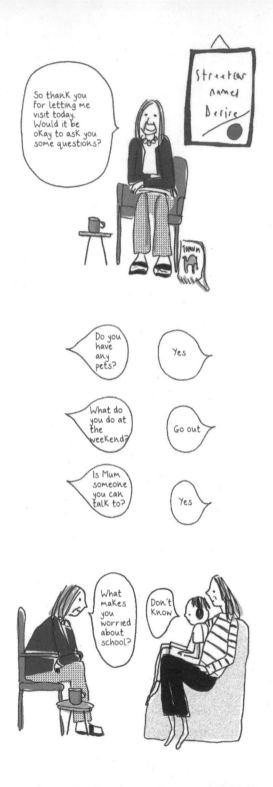

I still don't know who she was or what she did with that paperwork

'We don't take
children like that'

Realisation...

'What about
GCSEs?'

I have no idea who is meant to help with this. I thought if we had an EHCP it would mean something. No one has even checked on us. I don't know who is meant to take responsibility and make sure we get an education? I guess that only matters if it is easy and cheap and now it is more complicated everyone is just ignoring us. I should have fought more before to get what she needed, I should have tried harder... But what was I fighting for? I didn't know. But now what? What are we meant to do? Am I now left to try and teach her at home? What kind of message is that sending her? You are autistic but you should have tried harder to not be? I keep trying to make her feel okay and tell her it is okay but the bottom line is she's been left at home now. What is the future? What does it say about me as a parent that I couldn't make my child go to school like all the other children? I mean, lots of children have difficulties and manage to go to school so maybe it is my parenting. Maybe I should have been tougher and made her go? But I couldn't, she wouldn't, I didn't want to do that anymore and she wouldn't have gone anymore anyway. But what is the future? What will happen to her and us? Will it be all of us together, everyday, for evermore? What happens if something happens to me? Who will look after her? Who will fight for her? Who will understand her? But even I'm not that good at it because if I was, would we be in this situation? Meanwhile I need to be okay, for her because if I'm not then what will she think? What will everyone think? That I am a bad parent and that is why she can't go to school? I feel that everyone is scrutinising me and my personality. We created this. This situation. This enigma of a child who isn't doing what other children do. Who can't be helped. Maybe it is me? Which means I have to try even harder. I can't get things wrong. I must be better, try harder. But I am so tired and lost and worried. But I can't show it. I am needed. I don't want to go to any more sterile offices and talk about me, my family. I don't trust them, I don't know them. It's not like they do anything anyway. It is just their job and most of that seems to be to placate us because they can't do much else. It all makes me feel so exposed and mistrustful. I feel vulnerable because who really sees my family and wants to help? They just want to do everything within a ring fenced budget. How can we make a plan that works for us as a family when everything is about making her toughen up and go to bloody school? Shitty cardboard uniform, factory line school. Why can't she learn in a way that works for her not them? Who are all these people we have to navigate anyway? The job titles who pop in and pop off? They actually get paid for this and I have to spend all my time, unpaid emailing and waiting for phonecalls when I should and want to be with my child. I want to have a conversation when I am not talking or thinking about this. I used to think about other things. I used to have hobbies. Now I am an angry, bitter, boring special educational needs parent. I want to not feel guilty all the time, guilt I let my child down, guilt I used to shout to make her go to school, guilt I don't know how the hell this system works, guilt I let all these people talk me into stuff with my child when it all felt so wrong, guilt I am a shitty parent, guilt I am a boring friend and wife, guilt I can't work anymore... guilt guilt guilt guilt guilt guilt

'But how will she learn what real life is like?'

So I said

'We've done it their way for eight years, now we are doing it our way'

'You are more than a diagnosis and you are more than an institution'

Guidance and Thoughts for Schools and Professionals

by Sue Moon

Sue Moon is an independent speech and language therapist at Pebble Autism, a diagnostic service for children, adolescents and adults. Pebble Autism is committed to a neurodiversity-affirming approach which looks to provide a strengths-based assessment whilst adhering to National Institute for Health and Care Excellence (NICE) guidelines for assessment. Sue Moon also provides tailored training for schools, colleges and other organisations and professionals.

In this section, Sue provides specific guidance for schools supporting autistic pupils, with the aim of creating environments that reduce the risk of school avoidance. Many of the strategies she identifies will be relevant for pupils who do not have an autism diagnosis, but who are struggling in a formal learning environment.

First an important disclaimer... I am not autistic. These are my personal reflections based on some of the children, families, schools and professionals I have worked with.

I first became aware of Eliza on Twitter. Her beautifully observed sketches are some of the hardest-hitting and most acutely observed of all the neurodiversity-affirming content on social media. One tweet stood out for me, partly because of what it said about my profession (and others) and how it chimed with the ways my attitude to my job has changed over the years. A simple drawing of a child sitting at a desk was accompanied by the words: 'You can do all the courses and laminating in the world, you can collect certificates for training and do special days about mental health and autism, but ultimately what do you think it means to a child? What will they remember? The print outs or the person?' – Ouch!

In the three years it took me to qualify as a speech and language therapist we had less than a handful of lectures on autism. For me, a student placement in an adolescent Child and Adolescent Mental Health Services (CAMHS) in-patient unit was where the real learning started, not from books or lectures but from autistic people themselves. This experience also taught me that for some people there was a link between being autistic and developing mental health difficulties. What I didn't learn until later was that that link wasn't an inevitable consequence of being autistic, but the result of the way that autistic people are met by the world. I quickly realised that the lack of understanding and intolerance demonstrated by many non-autistic people was the source of much shame, trauma and distress for the people I worked with. I found myself day in day out listening to autistic teenagers who were bursting with empathy as they maturely, logically and compassionately appraised the confusing and often hurtful behaviour of their non-autistic peers. It wasn't the autistic kids who needed to be taught empathy and they weren't the ones who had poor social communication. They didn't need *fixing* at all.

At university we were taught that the phrase 'person with _____' was the respectful way of referring to clients. This was meant to acknowledge that a person was more than their disability. That by describing someone as 'autistic' we would prevent them from being anything other than that. Fast forward to a new decade where the narrative was being re-written by those *people with autism* who argued that being autistic actually *was* something that defined them. Suggesting they were a person *with* autism carried with it the assumption that they could, or should in some way, become a person *without* it. Late-diagnosed autistic adults also began sharing that much of what we professionals hired to 'help' had been doing, like teaching social skills, actually caused them harm. The rise of autistic voices in writing and research, and on social media, brought confirmation that my autistic clients were already whole people who didn't need therapy to make them less autistic. But my experience in the CAMHS unit taught me that they needed *something*. During this time, I was starting to notice that the therapy sessions that had the greatest impact on my clients were those where I listened without judgement, and where we created a climate in which they felt safe enough to begin to discover their own identity.

Years before that tweet of Eliza's, I was starting to understand the value of personal relationships over any therapy tools or techniques. When Eliza asked me for my thoughts on what schools could do to make autistic children's experiences more positive, I found myself thinking again about that tweet. I knew specific strategies weren't enough to guarantee that the school experience wouldn't be traumatic for autistic pupils. So instead, I wanted to somehow encourage everyone in schools to radically rethink their relationships with the autistic children they met. And one word kept coming into my head, *love*.

In a secular society we tend to think of love as something we reserve for our own children, our closest friends or our romantic partners, but showing love is one of the greatest gifts we can give anyone. There is a saying that *the children who need the most love will ask for it in the most unloving of ways*. Autistic pupils are some of the children in school who need the most love, yet they are often the ones who receive the least of it. From a young age, many will have become accustomed to feeling a disconnect between themselves and the world around them. If autistic children sense that the world is dangerous, unpredictable and confusing, they will develop ways of getting through each day. The resulting trauma-induced avoidant and reactive behaviours are all too often misinterpreted and even punished by the very people society trusts to protect and nurture its children. Many autistic children will try anything to fit in, by giving people what they feel is expected of them, or *masking*. Either one of these approaches, both a response to trauma, can, and often does, end in the child feeling unseen and misunderstood, and all too often leads to underachievement and poor mental health.

So, what do we mean by *love* and how can we demonstrate it in the classroom and the playground? How can schools ensure that every conversation they have about a child and every support strategy they implement is informed by an unconditional positive regard for their autistic pupils? This is different from and goes beyond concepts of autism *awareness* or *acceptance*. Being aware of and accepting autistic children still puts them into a category of otherness. If schools can see their autistic pupils as people first, with the same basic needs and human rights as their non-autistic counterparts, they will be closer to treating them with the unconditional positive regard that I have called *love*.

Many autistic children, if they have been officially identified, arrive at a new school accompanied by huge amounts of information. Some of this will be out of date because while information in documents like professionals' reports is static, children are not. It's so important that our autistic pupils are allowed to develop quality relationships in school with adults who really listen and respond to what they are told. Our children and their families are the best source of information we have and only when we are alert to what they are telling us can we truly ensure those children feel seen and heard. Schools that really value the autistic experience always stay curious about the ways in which school is contributing to what parents are experiencing at home, and work in a truly collaborative way with the whole family.

Not all children will tell us what we need to know using words, and some, although they can speak, will at times communicate with their emotions or their choices. It is our job to 'listen' with an open mind to all these forms of communication. We must be ready and willing to be wrong, feel comfortable in having our expectations challenged and learn to manage our difficult emotional responses when they are. Setting aside our assumptions and biases really allows us to listen out for what children and their parents want to tell us, not want *we* want or expect to hear.

Understanding and meeting communication, social and sensory needs is the most basic requirement for any school with an autistic child in their community. Knowing autistic pupils well and sharing information widely means that all the adults in school can predict situations that will be tricky and step in to remove them or make them more manageable. What works for non-autistic pupils may be the opposite of what the autistic child needs, so no matter how experienced school staff are, providing neurodiversity-affirming, autism-specific training and sharing excellent up-to-date information specific to the child is crucial.

However, even with the best quality up-to-date information to hand, the experience of school for many autistic children is exhausting and traumatic. Schools that feel safer are those that contain their pupils within a predictable environment where changes are minimal and explained in advance. There is also plenty that each of us can do on an individual level to make our autistic pupils feel safe. Adults that autistic children feel more relaxed around and start to trust are reliable because they do what they say they are going to do. They use calm and gentle voices and are clear and direct in their communication. They don't leave autistic children to work out what they mean from their facial expression, tone of voice and body language. They know that using humour can be the most wonderful way to forge strong relationships, help everyone relax and defuse difficult situations, but they are careful with the way they use it because they are aware that it can easily be misunderstood.

In many cases, the thing that is most likely to make autistic children feel safe is the knowledge that they have the option to escape. A truly calm and quiet place in school to retreat to when the classroom or playground gets too much is invaluable. It is helpful to have the option of adult support on hand, but important not to expect the child to communicate when they are in distress. Small escapes from work are important too; having an alternative activity on hand for those moments where the work feels impossible or before anxiety levels start to rise. This could be something the child enjoys, such as drawing or reading a book linked to a current interest. A well-timed switch of activity can de-escalate or even prevent a potentially explosive situation. To be truly effective, escape needs be totally unconditional and available on demand, not just when it's convenient to others.

In a school that values its autistic pupils, everyone understands what autism is and what it is not. Such schools foster a culture where being autistic isn't seen as a negative. Such schools embrace the neurodiversity of their student body and recognise the importance of timely diagnosis. Getting the right diagnosis can be hugely empowering and often comes to many children and families as a relief. In supportive schools, staff will know how to identify autistic children and will support them through diagnosis and beyond. They will create opportunities for autistic pupils to discover one another if this is appropriate because they understand that autistic children often 'get' one another and these schools recognise the power of knowing that you're not alone.

Great schools also find creative ways for autistic pupils to contribute and excel within the wider school community. They draw on their strengths, interests and passions but are always led by the preferences of each child. They take great care not to expose autistic children to situations where they will feel shame. They know not to put them in the spotlight without checking first, because things like being asked questions in class, being asked to read aloud, and receiving awards in assembly can be highly anxiety inducing.

Supportive schools do not expect academic and social development in line with non-autistic norms and they don't see a different rate of development as *less*. They look beyond exemplary behaviour and academic perfectionism and see the furious masking that is a ticking time-bomb for autistic burnout. They believe that sensory and communication adaptations are not luxuries for their autistic pupils, but necessities that put them on a more level playing field with their peers. They recognise that an autistic child may find the triple whammy of sensory, academic and social demands so tiring that a different kind of timetable is needed, and duvet days are required sometimes to avoid burnout. In acknowledging these differences and making adaptations without question, schools send a message that every child is valued as a person in all their beautiful human complexity.

Regardless of how many children there are at your school who have an autism diagnosis, it is likely that there are more who have yet to be identified. Learn about autism, get the certificates, but remember it is YOU who the child will remember. Make those memories good ones.

Reflections for Schools and Professionals

by Tom Vodden

A trained teacher, Tom Vodden has a background in mainstream and special education. He has taught in schools in England and Australia and run projects for young people permanently excluded from school.

Until recently Tom was one of the founding directors of the School Software Company and the originator of the Sleuth Tracking system – software designed to enhance schools' approaches to behaviour, safeguarding, attendance, and personal and social development.

Tom specialises in working with schools and organisations with a focus on behaviour, personal and social development, inclusion and SEND. He also delivers training with a focus on classroom management and supporting learners with neuro-developmental conditions.

Engaged by MATs, schools and other organisations as an improvement partner, Tom supports with strategic planning, organisation and staff development, project and change management.

*Tom holds an MEd in Psychology of Education and is currently study-
ing for an MSc in Occupational Psychology.*

*Tom is Co-Opted Governor for SEND at Bristol's largest autism special-
ist school, an SEN parent, occasional TES contributor, keynote speaker
and former member of the SEBDA National Council.*

I cannot think of another book of this length that says so
much, despite so very few words. The invitation to commit
more in writing than the author has throughout the preceding
pages is flattering but daunting.

These powerful and very personal biographical and autobiographical illustrations may be the windows through which
some readers see their family's lonely and painful personal
journeys. For others they offer an invaluable insight into a
completely unnavigable, emotional maelstrom – a storm
into which the lives of children and families are thrown
when school becomes a place that they CAN simply no
longer be.

Irrespective, these illustrations should make us pause and
reflect about how we might work collaboratively to make
education a place of safety again – for all the 'Lexys' out there.

The publication of this book comes at a time when increasing
numbers of children join the already too numerous 'ranks' of
the persistently absent. Or a step beyond, signed up members
of the 'elective home educated'. 'Elective' implies some kind
of choice, when, in reality, for the children who share the

experiences borne out in these illustrations, home education is the only remaining way to re-establish a safe space, an emotionally protective safe haven. To my knowledge there is no data readily available to allow us to understand the reasons for 'elective' home educating. There needs to be, with a box that can be ticked stating: 'left with no other choice'. Additional data like this would offer a broader starting point to better explore and understand just how inclusive education really is. There will be many among those numbers who feel excluded.

This book's publication comes at a time when schools regroup and recover after two years of a Covid pandemic. At a time when in England, in response to rising numbers of 'persistent absentees', a national attendance strategy has been launched – an initiative guided by a group with significant professional experience and expertise. However, it is a group that misses a critical and important voice. The Department for Education found no seat at the top table for the voices of parents and carers; nor did children themselves. For attendance strategies to succeed, collaboration, consultation, communication and a common understanding should sit at their core.

This book is important in that, while telling a very personal story, it communicates the shared experience of large numbers of families. Families with an insight and expertise that would enhance the work of any strategic body. It is also worth pointing out that while Covid has been identified as the trigger for a rise in persistent absenteeism, the reality is that pre-pandemic these numbers were already growing year on year. This begs the question: is the current response to concerns around attendance going to be solely rooted within and linked to the pandemic? For its impact to be far reaching, it must not be. That would be to avoid asking a broader-ranging set of questions. Questions that should encourage us to re-think and re-imagine the topography of the educational landscape in the UK. It is long overdue.

After over 25 years and counting in education in a variety of professional roles and as a parent, I cannot see how the narrative around attendance, or strategies by which 'acceptable' levels of attendance are 'achieved' has changed. Or at least not in any profound way. As I write, as if to helpfully illustrate my point, we are again seeing a 'new' strategy that includes fines for non-attendance. Fining parents, the 'hit them in the pocket' approach to tackling attendance issues, is a blunt tool, although it is a good headline-making one. It's a strategy that 'burns bridges' when making connections is key. In the current economic climate, we should also consider the financial hardship that may families face and the added stress that this adds. Change needs to come. Not to invite it is illogical – on many levels.

In this book it is the illustrations that carry and convey the weight of the narrative; however, it is the 'words in between', on the pages without illustration, that I'd like to use to extend and reflect on what I consider to be some of the key thinking points.

'All it needs to say is just being in school is enough'

As a parent I will not be alone in having heard the above words, or words conveying a similar sentiment. This is the point at which the school realises that simply getting into school will have involved a child drawing on such depths of determination and courage that learning is a virtual impossibility. The point when having spent all their energy ensuring their 'emotional safety', learning is not only impossible for these children but sadly has become irrelevant.

This is the point when 'stress exceeds support, when risks are greater than resilience and when "pull" factors that promote school nonattendance overcome the "push" factors that encourage attendance'.[1]

In reality, it is likely that any 'active' learning with any tangible intrinsic motivation fizzled out long before. It is at this point we have to ask ourselves where our priorities lie. When a child's attendance mark is of higher value than their engagement in learning, we have a problem. That problem, or a very significant part of it, would be addressed if we looked at the virtually irreconcilable competing priorities of school and home – a 'competition' over which neither has ultimate control but in which the performance of both will be judged.

Imagine for a moment the family for whom it is becoming a reality – the success of their child's education might be

---

1   M.S. Thambirajah, M.S., Grandison, K.J. and De-Hayes, L. (2008) *Understanding School Refusal*. London: Jessica Kingsley Publishers.

determined not by what they got out of school, but simply how many days they managed to get in. For balance, spare a thought too for the staff in the school whose careers are on the line if the call from Ofsted comes and their attendance marks don't cut the Department for Education mustard.

When I was teaching, I hadn't joined the profession to ensure children attended 95 per cent of the time. As a parent, my aspirations for my children were not that at 16 the success of their time at school might be measured by the amount of time they spent in school.

An 'in at all costs' approach to attendance comes at a significant price. To children, to parents and carers, and to schools and the professionals who work in them. It also constricts and narrows the possibilities as to how we can go about educating our children. Our shared efforts should not involve a fight to get children to attend – presenteeism is not 'attendance' and attendance figures do not indicate a child's emotional preparedness to learn – but to enable them to learn, to be educated and to be happy.

'All children have to go to school'

Do they? What do we mean by this? What does it say about our understanding of how children learn? What does it say about where they can learn? Does a school need a gate, desks, classrooms, bricks and mortar to educate children? Is there another way to get children 'through the school gate'? Is it not our priority to educate children, not simply to 'make them' go to school? Where school itself becomes a barrier to education is there no scope for flexibility?

In September 2021 a Department for Education official stated in working to address issues of attendance 'the school, family and council should work together to agree a plan for attendance, because the classroom is the best place for their education, development and wellbeing'.[2]

The period spanning the pandemic has seen schools, through the extraordinary determination, creativity and professionalism of their staff, re-imagine themselves, exist in a virtual environment and continue to educate their pupils. Our understanding of what classrooms can be like is beginning to shift.

When change is required, it can happen and can happen in a significant, rapid and impressive way. Sadly, and as pointed out by the parents and carers of many SEN children, this only becomes possible when the educational needs of the majority are at stake.

The kinds of solutions and alternatives we have seen over the period of the pandemic are actually the very solutions and alternatives from which children struggling with their attendance (predominantly SEND pupils) can benefit. With the pandemic came very real challenges for many children. However, for some children virtual learning, meant layers of challenge that come with school and learning within a

---

2   www.bbc.co.uk/news/education-58474418 (accessed 21 June 2022).

physical environment were stripped away. Specifically, for children with underlying neuro-developmental conditions, significant social and sensory barriers were almost immediately eliminated.

The successes and hard work of educational professionals teaching children during the pandemic should not be cast aside as we return to the 'new normal'. In the world of education, the 'new normal' needs to blend and synthesise. Continuing to use these approaches offers a chance to maintain the relevance of learning, which, for this group of children, is at risk of significant and long-lasting damage. Or, worse still, disappearing completely. They would offer a means to help children retain their connection with learning when struggling to maintain their connection with school as a physical environment because of its impact on their sense of 'emotional safety'.

In our evaluation of the successes of virtual learning we must not only look at how aspects of this might be retained, so as to extend provision, but, if we are to accept that 'the classroom is the best place for their education', we must also reflect on how 'the classroom' needs to change too because for SEND children, over-represented in attendance and exclusion data, there's enough to suggest it isn't.

I'm not persuaded that our idea of a traditional classroom is, for all children, 'the best place for their education, development and wellbeing'. Numerous illustrations throughout these pages challenge us to think more deeply about this.

'What about GCSEs?'

What about them? Well, along with attendance data, they can be seen to be equally damaging to children and families, like Lexy and her family, because of the pressure that comes with them. A common message, displayed across the walls of schools to motivate high attendance, is that with decreasing attendance comes the decreasing chance of securing successful results at GCSE. At the point at which children begin to struggle with attendance, I'm uncertain of the value of these messages. For children who have already begun to question their capacity for success in a school environment, who are likely to be making unhelpful comparisons with their peers, with a damaging impact on self-esteem, such messages will have an effect contrary to that intended. Such messages also implicitly suggest that children who struggle to attend don't want to learn and don't want to be successful. One might argue that also hidden within these 'motivational' messages is another insight into the pressure on schools and how they are, crudely, judged by results. These illustrations highlight a cultural narrative around attendance that needs to be re-imagined and challenged.

In addition, we need to re-think what we mean by lifelong learning and how we communicate this to our children; in particular, our expectation that children must sit public examinations against some kind of clearly mapped chronological timeline.

All is not lost if GCSEs aren't taken at the end of year 11, or A Levels at the end of year 13. But for families struggling to get their children into school, or even to find a school for their child, this is exactly how it can feel. It adds to the pressure, to the sense of being a parenting failure, as the more autobiographical illustrations suggest.

'No child wants to go to school'

Possibly not. But this book isn't a story of a child who didn't want to go to school. Nor is it the story of a family who didn't want her to go or try their utmost to get her there. It's the story of a child who couldn't, not wouldn't. Until we understand that, for a significant group of children, non-attendance is not a willful act, we will continue to get drawn into a battle of wills where alternative approaches are not seen to be required.

For some children school attendance is not a question of 'Will I or won't I?' but 'Can I or can't I?' Our approaches to supporting these children and their families need to continue to adapt to reflect this. Understanding non-attendance as an act of self-preservation not defiance is an important place to start.

The words of Bessel Van Der Kolk are worth pausing to consider, as they illustrate this succinctly: 'Despite the well documented effects of anger, fear and anxiety on the ability to reason many programs continue to ignore to need to engage the safety system of the brain before training to promote new ways of thinking'.[3]

---

3   Van der Kolk, B. (2015) *The Body Keeps the Score*. London: Penguin Books.

It might be the case that 'No child wants to go to school', but not all children will have hidden crying day after day before going in, or lay awake for hours on a Sunday night, or struggled with eating or suffered with physical illness triggered by anxiety. Not every family will be told to 'bring them in in their pyjamas' when their child cannot even contemplate getting dressed for school. We need to be mindful that the emotional state in which some children leave home each morning renders learning impossible and leaves parents and carers questioning themselves and what they are doing. It is important to consider that if children were to leave school fearing home, much as some children fear leaving home to go to school, then quite rightly we'd be implementing the requisite safeguarding measures.

Attendance should be about safety first, not standards and targets. Adapting our approaches and offering a more individualised response to accommodate need, in particular for SEND children, is not going to open the floodgates – a kind of 'Oh, if we do it for one, everyone will want that' response. Most children and their families just want to be the same and to fit in. When they can't fit in, we need to fit out. Often children understand the need for a more personalised approach better than adults do and are far more attuned to the needs of their peers.

The conversation about attendance has evolved; there are excellent examples of practice nationwide that are being developed to support anxious children. Books like this will continue this evolution in our understanding and response.

The bigger challenge will be to bring about a systemic shift that allows schools and families to work better together towards a shared goal, and to ask questions regarding the limitations of a standards agenda that requires a commonality and consistency of approach in order to be measured. Children don't fit neatly into boxes, but of course boxes are easy to count. A start would be to reflect on the language we use when discussing issues that relate to school attendance. Let's start with the phrase 'playing truant'. It's a term that makes school avoidance sound like a game that one party or another can 'win'. It's a phrase I thought had been 'retired' from the lexicon but appears to be making a return. For the families and children whose lives are reflected in these illustrations, non-attendance has never been a game. Such terminology over-simplifies 'non-attendance' when a 'triaged' approach is required; a more solution-focused 'needs-based' approach that moves beyond the simplification of a complex issue.

Too much of attendance strategy is reactive, focusing on what to do when children struggle to attend. A holistic and more considered approach requires us, or more specifically policy makers, to go back to the 'source of the river'; to explore what can be done to prevent children becoming persistently absent in the first place. Not to keep asking the question: how do we get them in? But having the courage to ask the question: what needs to change to prevent the issue in the first place? To reflect on the limitations and constraints of a standards agenda, at the heart of which sits attendance that focuses on numbers not children.

Afterword

Eliza Fricker

Thank you for letting me write and draw this.

You could have said no, because you (well, all of us) are quite private really.

And I suppose that fits well with this book because it is very much about one part of who you are.

Much of the time I would have loved them to see you, the real you, but it got lost.

Partly because you were so unwell you shut down and shut away but also partly because, post-diagnosis, they couldn't see beyond it.

You were the headphones, the egg timer and the smiley or sad faces.

And when that didn't work you became mainstream or special school.

And none of this fitted, because you were you.

I am still so dreadfully sorry for all those mornings I shouted at you when you were already so stressed, unhappy and unwell.

I was scared and worried for all of us.

I didn't want to get into trouble.

I didn't want to go to more meetings and not know the answers.

I didn't want to do it either.

What price did we all pay?

Many years of repair and restoration, because the truth is: eventually someone breaks.

There was a long time after all this at home.

Healing and reconnecting. Time, so much time, we had to start all over again.

But enough of all of that.

Let's talk about now. Wow!

We found a place, a place so different.

I still remember that morning I went with Dad to see it.

(With cynicism and fatigue.)

Here we go...

But I was so surprised, so relieved, when it became very clear that this place was different (even your dad, Mr Hold-Your-Horses, liked it straight away!).

This was about the each and every person, this was about healing and nurturing.

This was about learning through strengths.

Holistic, bespoke, child-led.

And what did they say? 'We'll take as long as it takes'.

Time.

'Thank you for trusting us with your family'.

Slowly, slowly.

I could let go. It was time to let go.

You want me to go.

And that feels very excellent indeed.

The Family Experience of PDA

An Illustrated Guide to
Pathological Demand Avoidance
Eliza Fricker
Illustrated by Eliza Fricker
Foreword by Ruth Fidler

£12.99 | $18.95 | PB | 144PP
ISBN 978 1 78775 677 9 | eISBN 978 1 78775 678 6

Eliza Fricker gets it. Describing her per-
fectly imperfect experience of raising
a PDA child, with societal judgements
and internal pressures, it is easy to feel overwhelmed, resentful and alone.
This book's comedic illustrations explain these challenging situations and
feelings in a way that words simply cannot, bringing some much-needed
levity back into PDA parenting. Humorous anecdotes with a compassion-
ate tone remind parents that they are not alone, and they're doing a great
job. If children are safe, happy and you leave the house on time, who cares
about some smelly socks?

A light-hearted and digestible guide to being a PDA parent covering
everything from tolerance levels, relationships and meltdowns to collaboration, flexibility and self-care to dip in and out as your schedule allows
to help get to grips with this complex condition.

This book is an essential read for any parent with a PDA child, to help
better understand your child, build support systems and carve out some
essential self-care time guilt free.

Eliza Fricker is an illustrator and a designer based in Brighton, UK. She
has a child with PDA.

I'm Not Upside Down, I'm Downside Up

Not a Boring Book About PDA

Harry Thompson and Danielle Jata-Hall

Illustrated by Mollie Sherwin

£9.99 | $14.95 | PB | 64PP

ISBN 978 1 83997 117 4 | eISBN 978 1 83997 118 1

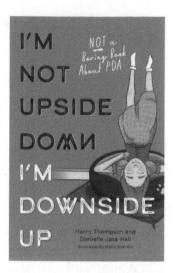

My name is Ariana and I have something called Pathological Demand Avoidance, which is a profile on the autism spectrum. Most people just think I'm naughty and misbehaved, but I want to show you why that's not true by telling you about what my life is like from inside my head. Come join me in understanding why I feel like I have to be in control all the time, and why it's just not as simple as doing as I'm told.

Harry Thompson is an Autistic PDA adult. He is the author of *PDA Paradox*, a public speaker, Autistic educator, PDA ambassador, consultant and self-advocate.

Danielle Jata-Hall is a parent of a PDA daughter and a blog writer at www.pdaparenting.com. She is a public speaker, PDA advocate and an online campaigner.

The Teacher's Introduction to Pathological Demand Avoidance

Essential Strategies
for the Classroom
Clare Truman

£14.99 | $21.95 | PB | 176PP
ISBN 978 1 78775 487 4 | eISBN 978 1 78775 488 1

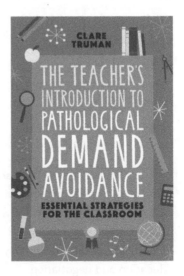

Being autistic, you might come across more challenges than others around you, such as dealing with ableism, discrimination in employment or difficulties in your relationships.

This essential guide for working with PDA pupils outlines effective and practical ways that teachers and school staff can support students, by endorsing a child-led approach to learning and assessment.

Beginning with an introduction to PDA and how it can affect the education experience, it is then followed by thoughtful, useful strategies school staff can implement to build a collaborative relationship with pupils and help them to thrive in the school environment. The activities presented aim to make children more comfortable and at ease, and therefore better able to learn.

Clare Truman has been a special needs teacher for eleven years, and specialised in autism for eight. In January 2017, she established Spectrum Space Community Interest Company, a social enterprise and alternative education provision which specialised in supporting children with a PDA profile.

Helping Your Child with PDA Live a Happier Life

Alice Running

£12.99 | $19.95 | PB | 128PP
ISBN 978 1 78775 485 0 | eISBN 978 1 78775 486 7

Drawing on the author's personal experience of parenting a child with PDA, this insightful and informative guide offers strategies and tips for all aspects of daily life, including sensory issues, education and negotiation.

Full of advice and support, this book is not intended to provide information on how to change your children. Rather, it is focused on creating the type of environment that will allow children to be authentically themselves, thereby enabling them to flourish and thrive.

Alice Running writes about autism (blogging and as a journalist) to create space for autistic voices. She has had articles published in *The Mighty*, *Yahoo*, *Special Needs Jungle*, *Huffington Post*, *Yorkshire Evening Post* and *The Big Issue* in the North. She is an autistic woman and has two sons with autism (one with PDA also).